Survival Guide:

10 Survival Skills That Will Help You To Survive In the Wilderness

Table of content

Introduction

This book is your first step towards becoming a professional and trained survivor. This book would not only develop your interest in survival skills but also help you learn the basics. If you are interested in learning some surviving skills and you don't know where to start, this is your ticket to learning some beginners stuff that would help you in learning more.

In this book, you will learn what kind of a mindset a survivor has. You can start training yourself on developing a psychology that is strong and that wants to survive no matter how hard surviving may seem.

After you get yourself acquainted with a survivor's mindset, I will share with you some really useful tips on finding the right food for your and how you can build a shelter for you. I would also help you set up your very own survival kit which is an interesting task.

After reading this book, you will be curious for more professional and expert stuff which would help you in getting properly trained as a survivor.

Chapter 1 - Psychology of Survival for Different Disasters

http://static1.squarespace.com/static/515cca87e4b0bca14d767b61/t/
55008126e4b0fc0ace81dc5b/1426096423043/Head+Scratch.png?format=300w

When you want to learn how you can survive in the wilderness, the first thing you should do is to learn the psychology of survival. By the psychology of survival, I mean how your mind works in survival situations, what is your attitude towards different life and death circumstances. If you start to panic, you would not be able to focus on the problem and this might cost you your life. In this chapter, I would discuss with you what survival is and how you can survive. After this, I will share with you four really important tips that would help you with developing a psychology that leads to survival in different disasters.

What do you know about survival?

First, you should know what survival is exactly. Survival is about deciding to live when circumstances are really harsh. To control your fears and emotions, not to be over confident in survival situations, is surviving.

If you know everything about different plants and herbs that you could eat in the wilderness and you know how to build a fire and how to find shelter for yourself etc but you don't know how to react when danger is near and you don't have the psychology of a survivor, you would not be able to survive. You should be decisive and a quick thinker if you really want to survive during different disaster situations.

No amount of survival knowledge would be enough to save you during harsh circumstances if you don't have a strong mindset.

TIP# 1: Develop the will to survive!

As discussed above, you can survive if you have a mentality, a psychology of a survivor. If your mind is always ready for difficult circumstances, you would survive. What is that helps people to survive even in the face of death? The **will to survive!** Survivors do not surrender to difficulties. They refuse to be defeated by harsh circumstances. They do not let the bad times decide what their fate will be. They choose for themselves. They choose their own fate. They live or they die trying. They never give up!

If you don't want to survive, you wouldn't. But if you have made up your mind that you will survive, not matter what, you will. Without having that **will to survive,** even the most expert survivors don't stand a chance. So the most important tip for your survival is your **will to survive.** Where there is a Will then there is always a way to fulfill that Will.

How does fear work?

In a difficult situation, the first emotion a human being deals with is fear. Now there are two kinds of psychologies of fear. Let's see what they are,

- The first psychology is when the fear takes over the mind. When this happens, the person loses his ability to think and react. Panic takes over and this results in the situation getting worse. Now this type of a mindset in a person can only make the circumstances worse.

- The second psychology of people is when they become hasty in the face of danger. They start to over think and over analyze the situation. And to get rid of the danger at hand, they make some hasty decisions that can lead to the situation becoming even worse than it was before. They let the fear blind them and they lose their ability to think clearly. And so they make wrong decisions that only increase the problem for them.

How can you stop fear from taking control?

To stop your fear of the dangerous situation taking over your mind, you have to be calm and not panic. Panicking is the worst thing you could do in the face of danger. Panic would only blind you. What do you need to do when the present situation builds fear in your mind?

TIP# 2: Take control of your mind and think rationally!

Fear can change the way you think. When you are afraid, your mind does things to you. You start panicking. Different negative thoughts start to run through your mind. This flow of thoughts hinders rational thinking and you become literally blind in the face of danger. You cannot conquer your mind if you don't think rationally in the face of danger. Even if thinking rationally means you are thinking about your death, do that. Use your rational thinking in helping you survive. If you know you can die in a bad situation, you would be able to do something about it. Just don't let your rational thoughts make you a coward. Your thoughts play a big role in handling any situation to think wisely and in a rational way to avoid any unexpected situation when you are in wild.

TIP#3: Do NOT panic and conquer your fear!

Control your mind and don't over think the situation. This is how you can take control of your mind. Stop for a second and calm your mind. Control the flow of your thoughts. Don't think too much. Just think about how you can get rid of the difficulty you are facing at that moment. Keep your calm, think rationally and do NOT panic because panic would be the death of you.

Do not surrender to your fears. Think about why the situation is scaring you and then think about how you can conquer your fear, how everything would seem easier if you can control your fear. If you give in to your fear, you would never survive.

TIP#4: Don't be overconfident and be a little afraid!

Now, you don't have to be overconfident. Many people die just because they were too over confident to even believe that the danger they are facing could harm them in any way. Let the situation scare you a little. It should be just enough to make you believe that you are not invincible, because everyone is invincible. Keep your ego in check that makes you think nothing could beat you. Be positive but not too much!

These four tips are the most important things you will learn in this book because if you have learned the psychology of survival, you can beat anything that comes between your survival and you. If you train yourself into utilizing the four most important tips, you can rest assured that no situation, it doesn't matter how difficult it is, can beat you! Just remember, you need the "will to survive" and to "take control of your mind."

Chapter 2 - Essentials of Survival Kit

In this chapter, you would learn about what you should have in your survival kit when you are stuck in the wilderness. I would give you two tips on how you can make the perfect survival kit for you to help you out in the wilderness and when you are stuck in a survival situation.

TIP# 5: Add first-aid items in your survival kit!

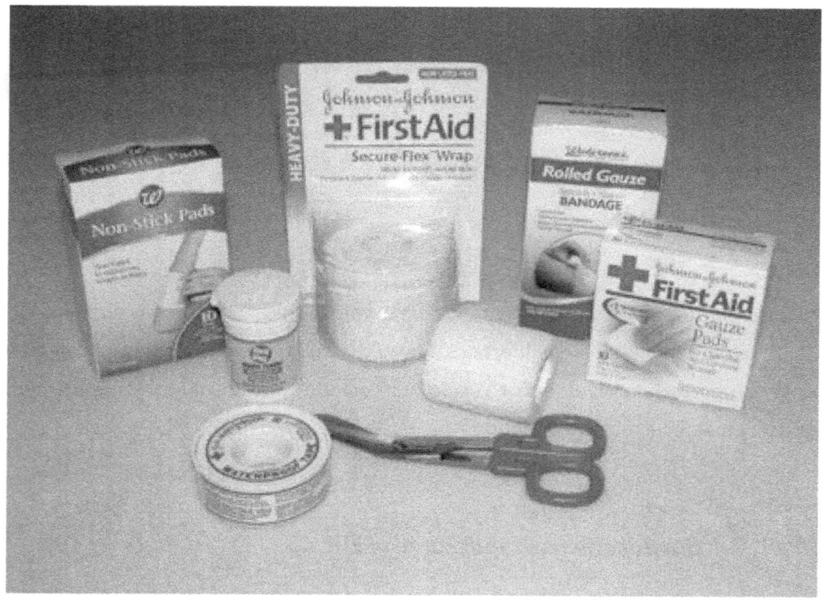

http://blog.petmeds.com/wp-content/uploads/2012/11/Kit3-1024x768.jpg

What would happen if you are wounded in the middle of nowhere? How can you help yourself if you have no one to go to and no one to ask for help? In situations like these, you should add some basic and really important first aid items to your survival kit. The items you would need to add in your survival kit that would help you when you are injured or ill are as follows,

- A water bottle - To drink or to clean up your wounds or injuries

- Adhesive tape – For keeping the splints and dressing intact

- Cotton balls and cotton buds – For applying ointments or other medications to different injuries

- Absorbent cotton rolls - To serve as a padding for splints

- Aluminum finger splint

- Eye pads

- Bandage strips (Different sizes) – For major and minor cuts

- Butterfly bandages - For holding the cuts together to heal up

- Roller gauzes (Different sizes) – To give support to sprained muscles or sore body parts

- Sterile gauze pads – For wounds that keep bleeding or for secretion and also to keep the injuries from catching germs or bacteria

- Petroleum jelly

- Instant cold packs – To use on contusions or bruises

- Plastic bags (Different sizes)

- Tweezers

- Safety pins (Different sizes)

- Scissors

- Face and dust masks - To protect against dust, germs or allergens

- A First-aid manual

After you have gathered all these supplies, get the following medications to put in your survival kit,

- Cough and cold medications

* Pain relievers

* Eyewash solution

* Antibiotic ointment - To prevent different injuries from festering

* Antiseptic solution - To clean your injuries

* Antacids - For Acid Reflux

* Aloe vera gel – For healing your wounds

* Calamine lotion – To apply on burns and rashes or to relieve pain and to prevent itching

* Medication for diarrhea

* Laxative - For increasing bowel movements

* Antihistamine - For allergies

* Hydrocortisone cream - To cure chemical reaction on skin

Other non-medical things that you should keep in your survival kit all the time are,

* A water resistant flashlight

* Waterproof matches

* Insect repellents

* Sun block

Now that you have the necessary medical equipment and supplies, you need some other things in your survival kit too. That is the next tip.

TIP# 6: Add forager toolkit to your survival kit!

https://naterunals.files.wordpress.com/2012/08/group.jpg?w=500&h=333

Why would you need a forager toolkit? When you are stuck in the wilderness and you have nothing to eat, you would have to find food for yourself. But for that, you should have some basic knowledge about what to eat and what not to, in the wilderness. I will discuss that briefly in the next chapter. Your forager toolkit should have the following items,

Transport containers:

Your forager toolkit should have different containers for different sorts of food that you would find in the wilderness. When you find different eatable herbs, plants or fruits in the wilderness, you would want to take them back to your shelter. For this, you should have different kinds of containers with you in your forager toolkit. You should have the following transport containers with you,

- Plastic bags – For collecting herbs and plants in big quantities

- Sandwich bags – For collecting seeds and nuts or other tiny things

- Freezer bags – For larger plants like sumac

- Covered containers – For fruits and berries that might get crushed in bags

Different picking aids:

You have to have some items that you would need to help you to pick different fruits and plants. You can have the following picking items in your survival kit,

- A pair of scissors – For cutting thorny plants that you can't pick with your hands

- Gardening gloves – For picking up thorny fruits like stinging nettles

- Cardboard mitts – For picking up thorny fruits whose thorns tear the gardening gloves too

- A long stick – To shake the branches of long trees to get the fruit to fall down

- Mini hand trowel – To dig the plants whose roots you could eat too.

If you follow the 2 tips mentioned in this chapter, you would be ready for any emergency situations in the wilderness. If you are hungry and you don't have enough food, you could collect food from nature all by yourself. You just have to know what to eat and what not to. The medical kit and the forager toolkit are absolutely necessary for your survival kit. They would help you a lot when you are stranded in the wilderness.

Chapter 3 - Survival Skills in Wilderness to Search Food

In this chapter, I would give you 2 more tips about searching food in the wilderness. You cannot survive in the wilderness without food. If you don't have anything to eat, you would have to find it in the wilderness. And I can tell you, you could find so much to eat in nature. You just have to look for the right food.

TIP# 7: Know some plants and herbs that you can find in the wilderness

You should know about different plants and herbs that you can find in the wilderness to eat. For that, you would need to learn some basic foraging skills. But in this chapter, I would tell you about some of the herbs and plants in the wild that you can eat and I would share their pictures too for you to recognize those plants.

1. **Amaranth:**

You can recognize the weed from the above picture. You can eat this plant raw if the situation is really bad. But it is recommended that you boil the weed before you eat it to remove the oxalic acid and nitrates from it.

2. **Asparagus:**

This vegetable looks like this:

http://content.artofmanliness.com/uploads//2010/10/asperagus.jpg

You can eat this raw or boil it. It is rich in vitamin B6, potassium, thiamine and vitamin C.

3. **Burdock**:

http://content.artofmanliness.com/uploads//2010/10/burdock.jpg

You can eat this plant raw too but this is a bitter plant and you can boil it two or three times to remove the bitter taste before you eat it. It is very popular in Japan. The leaves and stalks of this plant can be eaten.

4. **Cattail:**

http://content.artofmanliness.com/uploads//2010/10/cattails.jpg

This plant is also called punks and bullrush. It is found near wetlands. The rootstock, rhizomes of this plant is eatable too. Just wash off all the mud from this plant. The white part of this plant is the best part. You can eat it raw or you can boil it, however you want.

5. **Clovers:**

You can find clovers in grassy areas. They can be recognized by their trefoil leaflets. They can be eaten raw but it's better if you boil them first.

6. **Chicory:**

http://content.artofmanliness.com/uploads//2010/10/chicory.jpg

This plant is found in Europe, North America and Australia. Most of this plant is eatable. The flowers are really tasty and can serve as a quick snack for you.

7. **Chickweed:**

http://content.artofmanliness.com/uploads//2010/10/chickweed.jpg

This herb is found in the temperate and arctic zones. The leaves are rich in vitamins and minerals and you can eat them raw or you can boil them before you eat them.

8. **Curled Dock:**

The stalk of this plant can be eaten raw or boiled before eating. Just make
sure you have peeled off the first layer. This plant is bitter so it's better if

you boil it to remove the bitterness. This plant is found in Europe, North and South America and Australia.

9. **Dandelion:**

This weed is often found in your lawn. But in the wild, you can eat this plant to survive. You can eat the entire plant, the roots, leaves and the flowers. Younger leaves are better because fully grown leaves are bitter. You would need to boil them first. Roots can be eaten too.

10. **Field Pennycress:**

This weed is found in most parts of the world. The seeds and leaves of this plant can be eaten. If this plant is growing in contaminated soil, do NOT eat it.

TIP#8: Know the Do's and the Don'ts of collecting food from the wild!

If you are stuck in the wild and you have to collect food to eat from the wild, there are a few things that you should keep in mind,

The Do's,

- **Get help from an expert.** It is important that you get help from a foraging expert who can guide you and teach you how to recognize different plants and herbs.

- **Learn about the origin of various eatable plants.** When you are stuck in the wilderness, you cannot just go and look for any plant there. What if the plant that you are looking for grows in wetlands while you are stranded in a mountainous region?

- **Learn about companion plants.** These are the plants that grow with their poisonous companions. For example, you are looking for morel mushrooms and when you find them, you would find their non-edible companion plants too. Make sure you know that the companion plants are not to be eaten.

- **Make sure that you are not collecting a look-a-like of an eatable plant.** There are plants that look exactly alike but one is eatable while the other is poisonous or non-eatable. In such cases, smell the plants, feel the texture and make sure you are selecting the right plant to eat.

- **Use all of your senses.** Don't just believe your eyes because the plant that you have found may look like the eatable plant you know about but it may not be so. Make sure you observe minutely, smell the plant and feel its texture.

- **Make sure you know which part of the plant is eatable.** There are plants that are entirely eatable. But there are some plants who's some parts can be eaten only. Be sure you know the details.

The don'ts:

- **Don't eat anything that you are not sure about.** If you are not sure that the weed or plant that you are going to eat is safe to eat or not, don't eat it. Don't guess about things you find in the wild.

- **Don't destroy the whole plant when you only need is one part.** We know that you can be frustrated in the wilderness but the best thing is to keep calm. So keep your calm when you have found a plant that you can eat. Don't, in your haste, break the whole plant. Be patient and delicate with the plants. Collect only the parts that you could eat. Let the rest of the plant intact so that it can keep growing.

- **Don't eat from the plants that are unhealthy.** Plants can get certain diseases too. So if you have found an eatable plant but it looks unhealthy, leave it. Plants are sometimes affected by pests and fungi. Don't eat those plants. Collect the plants that look completely healthy and are not affected by any germs or bacteria.

If you keep the two tips discussed in this chapter in mind, you would be able to eat safe food in the wilderness. There are many poisonous plants that grow in the wilderness but if you take care of these two tips, you would be eating safe when you are stuck in the wild.

Chapter 4 - Survival Skills for Shelter

<https://boyslifeorg.files.wordpress.com/2014/04/survival-shelter.jpg?w=620>

In this chapter, I would give you two final tips that are related to shelter. When you are stranded in the wilderness and you don't know how long it would be until someone realizes that you have been gone for too long and they come for your help, you need to decide how you are going to survive in the wilderness. It might take the rescue days to find about your whereabouts, even months. You cannot just sleep in the open for that long, can you? For this, it is necessary that you find a proper shelter for yourself. If you cannot find a proper shelter, you have to make one for yourself. In this chapter, I would tell you how you can make different shelters when you have nothing to build a shelter from.

TIP# 9: Find a proper place to build your shelter.

First thing is to find a proper space where you can build a shelter for yourself. Keep the following points in mind when looking for the right spot to build up your shelter on:

- **The space should not be damp:** If anything that sucks up all the heat from your body fast, it's wetness. Make sure you have found the driest place in the wilderness to build up your shelter on. Building a shelter on wetland would result in you getting a fever and losing your body temperature.

- **Choose a high ground to build a shelter on:** You should look for a high ground for yourself if the weather isn't too cold. The breeze on the higher ground would save you from different bugs and mosquitoes. Plus higher ground will more secure for you. And if any search parties are coming, you would be able to see them easily from the top.

- **Choose a place sheltered place by trees if the weather is cold:** You can keep yourself from cold winds in a place that is covered with trees. The trees would block the cold winds and they would keep you warm too. Make sure you don't find the trees in a deep valley or ravine because cold winds settle down at night and in a valley it would be much colder.

- **Choose a spot that is nearer to a water spring:** You don't expect to survive in the wild without easy access to water. For this, it is better to find a place from where you could easily walk to the spring to drink water or to clean yourself up. Water is important. Most deaths happen in the wilderness because of dehydration. To ensure you get water all day and night, finding a spot near a spring would be a wise decision.

TIP#10: *Know how to build different shelters.*

You should know how you can build yourself a nice shelter to sleep in at nights and stay in the day. Here are some easy shelters that you can make when you have nothing with you to make a shelter from.

- **The cocoon:**

https://boyslifeorg.files.wordpress.com/2008/01/cocoon.jpg?w=620

It's your first night in the wilderness and you have done nothing about a shelter because you thought you could find a way out but you didn't. This is the quickest and the easiest shelter you could make for yourself. Collect the debris from the forest and make a pile from it. It should be two to three feet high from the ground and it should be longer than your height. Snug into this shelter and it will work as a sleeping bag and prevent your body from losing heat.

- **The fallen tree:**

https://boyslifeorg.files.wordpress.com/2008/01/fallentree.jpg?w=620

This shelter is also really easy and quick to make. Find a fallen tree that is big enough for you to lie inside it. Now lean the branches of the fallen tree to make a wall in such a way that the wind doesn't blow against it. Make sure the wall is thick enough so the wind doesn't get it. You can build a small fire on the open side of the shelter to keep you warm

- **The lean-to:**

https://boyslifeorg.files.wordpress.com/2008/01/leanto.jpg?w=620

If there is a tree that doesn't have enough space for you to crawl in, you can build a lean-to shelter for yourself. You can do so with a small rock or an overhang too. Lean fallen branches against the object to create a wall. To shield from the rain, lean the branches at a certain angle. Cover the branches with leaves, pines and other debris you could find. Get under the shelter when the wall is thick enough to protect you from the cold. Don't build your shelter too big for you to fit in. The bigger the shelter is, the more difficult would it be to keep it warm. Just make a shelter you could lie in.

There is another way you could build a lean-to shelter for yourself. Place one end of a long stick on the low limb of a tree and prop up the other end of the stick with 2 more sticks. Use your shoelace or belt to tie up the ends of the 2 sticks that you have added. Now lean more limbs against the stick and form a structure. Now use the debris, leaves, and pines and pile them up on the structure that you have made. Make a thick layer of debris so that no heat could come in or leave the shelter. You can build a small fire for you at the open end to keep yourself warmer. The fire would make the lean-to warmer.

- **The A-frame:**

https://boyslifeorg.files.wordpress.com/2008/01/a_frame.jpg?w=620

If you cannot make a lean-to, you could always make an A-frame shelter. Find two sticks that are 4 to 5 feet long and one more stick that is twice longer than the other two. Put the smaller sticks in such a way that you form an "A" with them. Now put the longer stick on top of this "A". Use your belt or shoelace to tie the three sticks together where they meet each other. You have now formed an A-frame tent-like structure. One end of this structure is collapsed on the ground. Now find more small sticks and prop them against the longer stick to form shorter "A". Now cover the structure with debris and make a thick wall. Make sure the debris covers the structure completely and the shelter is thick enough to keep you warm.

- **A tarp:**

https://boyslifeorg.files.wordpress.com/2008/01/tarp.jpg?w=620

You can make this shelter if you have a tarp with you or a plastic sheet or a blanket may be. This is really easily if you have any of these things with you. Tie your shoelaces together and toe one end to one tree and its other end to another tree nearby. Hang the tarp or the plastic sheet on the shoelace that you have tied to the trees. Now collect some rocks and fix the ends of the tarp or the plastic sheet in place using the rocks. This emergency tent would help you to stay warm. You can build a fire nearby to keep yourself from losing body temperature.

These were the last two really important tips that you should follow if you are trapped in the middle of nowhere. These shelters are not only easy to make, they are really helpful in keeping you warm. Just find the right place for you to set up your shelter and then choose from the above types of different emergency tents according to your needs and the nature of the place you are lost in.

Conclusion

In this book, you have learnt how to survive if you are stranded in the wilderness. This book is important because you don't know when you are stuck somewhere. You have to learn these 10 survival skills and train for any emergency situations. You don't know when you would need these skills.

This book would help anyone who wants to survive the difficulties one faces in the wilderness where you cannot get help from anyone and you are your own rescue. For situations like this, you have to be self-sufficient and this book is about learning how to be self-sufficient. You don't know when someone would come to your rescue. It could be days, even months. Until that happens, you have to rely on these skills.

If you have understood the psychology of survival, how you can control your fear and use your fears in a positive way, you would not need any rescuing. If you have the will to survive, you will survive or you will die trying.

The survival kit I talked about in the 2nd chapter is an essential part of your survival. You should always keep it with you.

You cannot think of surviving in the wild without nutritious food and proper shelter. I have tried my best to help you with these skills too. If you have read this book and understood the ideas, you would be able to survive any difficult situations.

FREE BonusReminder

If you have not grabbed it yet, please go ahead and download your special bonus report *"DIY Projects. 13 Useful & Easy To Make DIY Projects To Save Money & Improve Your Home!"*

SimplyClicktheButtonBelow

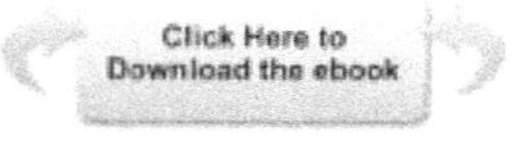

OR **Go to This Page**

http://preppersliving.com/free http://preppersliving.com/free

http://preppersliving.com/free

BONUS #2: More Free & Discounted Books

Do you want to receive more Free & Discounted Books?

We have a mailing list where we send out our new Books when they go free or with a discount on Kindle. Click on the link below to sign up for Free & Discount Book Promotions.